Corals

Science Under The Sea

Lynn M. Stone

Rourke

Publishing LLC
Vero Beach, Florida 32964

PHOTO CREDITS: Cover, p. 10, 12, 13, 15, 16, 19 © Marty Snyderman;title page,
p. 4, 7, 8, 20 © Brandon Cole;

Cover Photo: *Soft Coral polyps*

EDITOR: Frank Sloan

COVER DESIGN: Nicola Stratford

Library of Congress Cataloging-in-Publication Data

Stone, Lynn M.
  Corals / Lynn M. Stone.
     p. cm. — (Science under the sea)
Summary: Describes the physical characteristics, behavior, habitat, and
life cycle of these tiny sea creatures, some of which build coral reefs.
Includes bibliographical references (p.).
  ISBN 1-58952-318-0 (hardcover)
  1. Corals—Juvenile literature. [1. Corals. 2. Coral reefs and
islands.] I. Title.
  QL377.C5 S76 2002
  593.6—dc21

                                          2002005128

Printed in the USA

CG/CG

Table of Contents

Giant Structures

The biggest structures made by animals are not giant eagle nests or towering termite hills. They are the **coral reefs** of the world's warm oceans.

Corals are little animals, but the reefs they build are huge structures. Living coral reefs are hard, jagged undersea platforms of rock. Some of them spread out for miles.

This is the outer edge of a shallow coral reef surrounding an island in Indonesia.

A Simple Animal

Hundreds of different kinds of sea animals find food and shelter on reefs. In building their own homes, corals build homes for other animals, too.

The coral animal is what scientists call a **polyp**. A polyp is basically a soft, fleshy bag with **tentacles**. It is a simple animal with no eyes, ears, brains, or bones. Like a bag, a coral polyp has an opening only at one end. A polyp's opening, its mouth, is ringed by its finger-like tentacles.

Coral communities are hiding and feeding places for other animals.

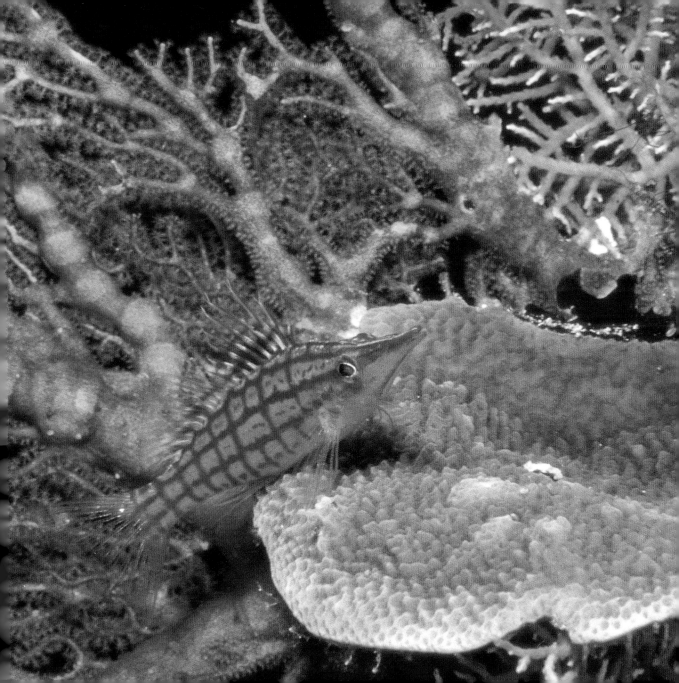

The Coral's Weapons

The animal's round mouth ringed by the soft, waving tentacles makes many corals look like sea flowers. But the tentacles aren't nearly as gentle as they seem. Like the tentacles of sea anemones and jellyfish (coral cousins), coral tentacles are loaded with tiny stingers. Tentacles are the coral's weapons.

While feeding, palm coral polyps look like white flowers.

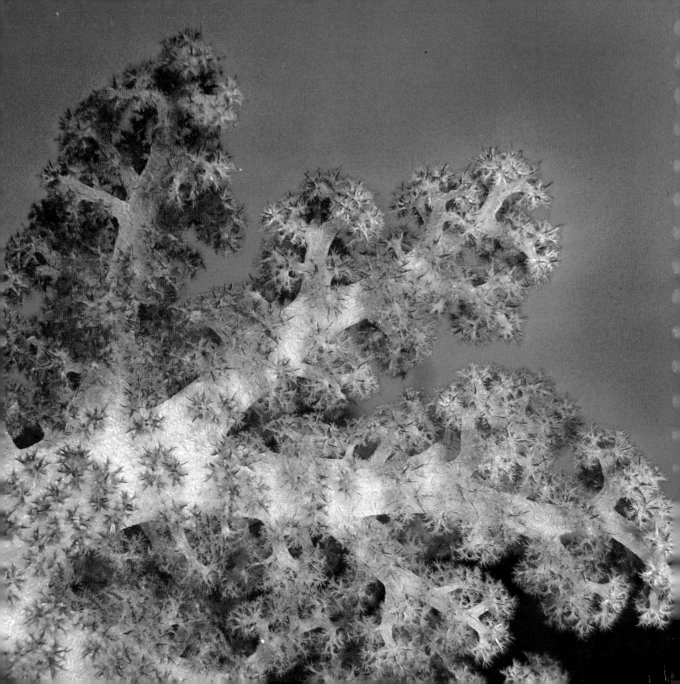

Stony and Soft Corals

Not all **species** of coral make reefs or live in warm seas. Corals of one kind or another live throughout the oceans.

Scientists often refer to some corals as "stony" and others as "soft."

Soft coral polyps come out of their skeletons to feed at night.

The tentacles around mouths of feeding coral polyps carry deadly stings for small sea animals.

Colorful parrotfish feed on both coral polyps and skeletons.

Building Reefs

All coral polyps are soft. However, stony corals can take certain materials from ocean water and change them to another form. A stony coral polyp, for example, can make a pasty material that hardens into a limestone cup.

The rocky cup is the polyp's house and outside skeleton. Simple animals like corals don't have inside skeletons.

Colonies of brain coral polyps make hard, round skeletons that look like human brains.

Corals in Colonies

Many stony corals live in **colonies**. Colonies are whole groups of animals living close to each other. A colony of stony coral polyps makes limestone skeletons that harden together. The colony shares a skeleton. Each polyp has its own cup or hole in the skeleton.

Over a long time, the limestone skeletons of many colonies become a reef. New coral polyps continue building the reef.

Each of these coral polyps lives in its own small part of the colony's hard skeleton.

A Variety of Reefs

   Amazingly, king-size coral reefs are built by polyps that are thumb-sized and even smaller.

   Stony corals build structures of amazing variety. The common names of many corals tell what they look like. Some of these names include brain, rose, star, staghorn, and lettuce-leaf.

Elkhorn coral got its name from its antler-like branches.

Soft Corals

Some soft coral polyps form flabby, jellylike masses. Another group of soft corals builds skeletons that look like fans, whips, and feather plumes.

These corals wave in sea currents like branches in the wind. They're made largely of a **protein** substance. They're flexible, like soft plastic. They don't build reefs, but they grow on reefs.

Sea fans, sea whips, and sea feathers are among the soft corals growing on this colorful coral reef in Fiji.

Predator and Prey

Sooner or later, tiny sea animals drift against a coral polyp's tentacles. The coral's tentacles then release deadly, dart-like threads. The tentacles kill or injure **prey**. The tentacles bring the prey into the polyp's mouth.

Because they eat other animals, corals are **predators**. But corals are also prey for such animals as butterfly-fish and parrotfish.

Glossary

colonies (CALL uh neez) — gatherings of animals of the same kind; the place where animals gather

coral reefs (KOR uhl REEFS) — huge, undersea limestone structures made by the skeletons of stony corals

polyp (PALL ip) — a fleshy, baglike animal with a row of tentacles around its mouth

predators (PRED eh torz) — animals that hunt other animals for food

prey (PRAY) — an animal hunted by other animals

protein (PROH teen) — an important natural substance needed for the growth of living things

species (SPEE sheez) — within a group of closely related animals, one certain kind, such as *staghorn* coral

tentacles (TEN te kelz) — soft, finger-like structures used by polyps to grasp, cripple, and kill prey

Index

Further Reading

Cerullo, Mary M. *Coral Reef: A City That Never Sleeps.* Dutton Children's Books, 1996
Owens, Caleb. *Coral Reef.* Childs World, 1998
Taylor, Barbara. *Coral Reef: A Close-Up Look at the Natural World of a Coral Reef.*
    Dorling Kindersley, 1992

Websites To Visit

Corals and Anemones: http://www.seasky.org/reeflife/sea2b.html

About The Author

Lynn Stone is the author of more than 400 children's nonfiction books. He is a talented natural history photographer as well. Lynn, a former teacher, travels worldwide to photograph wildlife in its natural habitat.